Connected Hearts

How Effective Communication Transforms Relationships

DALE JORDAN

© Copyright 2024 by DALE JORDAN

All Rights Reserved

The presentation of the information is without contract or any type of guarantee assurance. The trademarks that are used are without any consent, and the publication of the trademark is without permission or backing by the trademark owner. All trademarks and brands within this book are for clarifying purposes only and are the owned by the owners themselves, not affiliated with this document.

Table of Contents

Chapter 1

Introduction

The Power of Communication in Relationships

Communication is the lifeblood of any relationship. Whether it's a romantic partnership, a friendship, or a professional connection, the ability to share thoughts, feelings, and intentions effectively can make or break the bond. Effective communication fosters understanding, trust, and cooperation, while poor communication can lead to misunderstandings, conflict, and a breakdown in the relationship.

One key aspect of effective communication is active listening. This involves more than just hearing the words spoken by the other person; it means fully engaging with the speaker, understanding their message, and responding thoughtfully. Active listening requires concentration and a genuine interest in the other person's perspective. It's about being present in the moment, making eye contact, and showing empathy. By nodding, summarizing what was said, and asking clarifying questions, you demonstrate that you value the other person's input.

Non-verbal communication also plays a crucial role in how we connect with others. Body language, facial expressions, and tone of voice can all convey emotions and attitudes that words alone might not fully express. For instance, crossed arms can signal defensiveness, while a warm smile can indicate openness and friendliness. Being aware of your own non-verbal signals and interpreting those of others can enhance your ability to communicate effectively.

Transparency and honesty are fundamental to building trust in any relationship. When you communicate openly and honestly, you show that you respect the other person and value the relationship. This means being truthful even when it's difficult, admitting mistakes, and expressing your feelings and needs clearly. However, honesty should be tempered with tact and sensitivity. It's important to deliver difficult messages in a way that is respectful and considerate of the other person's feelings.

Conflict is an inevitable part of any relationship, but how you handle it can determine whether it strengthens or weakens the bond. Effective communication during conflict involves staying calm, listening to the other person's perspective, and expressing your own views without blame or hostility. It's about finding common ground and working together to resolve the issue. Avoiding accusatory language and instead using "I" statements can help to keep the conversation constructive. For example, saying "I feel hurt when you do this" is more effective than "You always do this to hurt me."

Another aspect of communication that can enhance relationships is expressing appreciation and gratitude. Regularly acknowledging and appreciating the positive qualities and actions of the other person can strengthen the bond and create a positive atmosphere. This can be as simple as saying "thank you" or expressing specific compliments. When people feel valued and appreciated, they are more likely to reciprocate those positive feelings.

Setting boundaries is also a crucial part of healthy communication in relationships. Boundaries define what is acceptable and unacceptable behavior and help to protect your emotional well-being. Communicating your boundaries clearly and respectfully can prevent misunderstandings and resentment. It's important to be assertive but not aggressive when setting boundaries, and to respect the boundaries of others.

Empathy is another powerful tool in communication. Empathy involves putting yourself in the other person's shoes and understanding their feelings and perspectives. This doesn't mean you have to agree with them, but it does mean acknowledging their emotions and showing that you care. Empathy can help to de-escalate conflicts, build trust, and deepen the emotional connection in a relationship.

Effective communication is also about being mindful of cultural differences. Different cultures have different communication styles, norms, and expectations. Being aware of these differences and adapting your communication style accordingly can prevent misunderstandings and foster mutual respect. This might involve adjusting your language, tone, or body language to align with cultural norms.

In romantic relationships, communication is key to maintaining intimacy and connection. This involves not only talking about everyday matters but also sharing your hopes, dreams, fears, and desires. Open and honest communication about your needs and expectations can prevent misunderstandings and ensure that both partners feel heard and valued. Regular check-ins and quality time together can help to maintain the emotional connection and keep the relationship strong.

In friendships, communication helps to build and maintain trust and loyalty. This involves being there for each other in times of need, sharing experiences, and supporting each other's goals and dreams. Good friends communicate openly and honestly, offer constructive feedback, and are willing to listen and empathize. They also respect each other's boundaries and accept each other's differences.

In professional relationships, effective communication is essential for collaboration, productivity, and a positive work environment. This involves clear and concise communication, active listening, and constructive feedback. It's important to communicate your expectations, provide regular updates, and address any issues promptly and professionally. Building strong professional relationships also involves showing appreciation for your colleagues' contributions and respecting their ideas and perspectives.

Technology has transformed the way we communicate, offering new opportunities and challenges. While digital communication can be convenient and efficient, it can also lead to misunderstandings due to the lack of non-verbal cues. It's important to be mindful of how you use technology in your relationships and to ensure that it enhances rather than hinders communication. This might involve using video calls for more personal interactions, being clear and concise in written communications, and avoiding misunderstandings by clarifying any ambiguities.

Effective communication is a skill that can be developed with practice and effort. It requires self-awareness, empathy, and a willingness to listen and understand. By focusing on improving your communication skills, you can enhance your relationships and build stronger, more meaningful connections with others. Whether it's through active listening, expressing appreciation, setting boundaries, or navigating conflicts, the power of communication lies in its ability to create understanding, build trust, and foster a sense of connection and belonging. Understanding the significance of communication in relationships also involves recognizing and addressing barriers that can impede effective interaction. These barriers can take many forms, including emotional, psychological, and environmental factors that interfere with the clear exchange of ideas and feelings.

Why Communication Matters

Communication weaves the fabric of human interaction, making it foundational to the way we understand and relate to each other. The importance of communication transcends mere information exchange; it is the vessel through which relationships are nurtured, conflicts are resolved, and progress is made. Mastering the art of communication can profoundly impact personal and professional spheres, making it a skill worth cultivating.

Imagine a world where every intention and emotion could be perfectly conveyed and understood. While this ideal is unattainable, honing communication skills brings us closer to it. Effective communication involves clarity, empathy, and active listening, each playing a pivotal role in ensuring that messages are not just sent but also received and understood as intended.

Clarity in communication eliminates ambiguity and confusion. When articulating thoughts, whether in a casual conversation or a formal presentation, choosing precise words and structuring sentences logically helps convey the message accurately. Consider the difference between saying, "We need this done soon," versus, "We need this report completed by Friday at noon." The latter leaves no room for misinterpretation, clearly stating the expectation.

Empathy is the cornerstone of meaningful communication. It requires putting oneself in another's shoes to understand their feelings and perspectives. Empathy bridges gaps that logic alone cannot. When someone shares their struggles, responding with empathy—such as acknowledging their feelings and offering support—can foster deeper connections and trust. This emotional resonance is critical in personal relationships and can transform professional interactions by creating a more collaborative and compassionate work environment.

Active listening goes beyond hearing words; it involves engaging with the speaker, reflecting on their message, and responding thoughtfully. It requires full attention, free from distractions, and genuine interest in what the other person is saying. Techniques like nodding, maintaining eye contact, and summarizing key points show the speaker that their message is valued. Active listening validates the speaker's experience and encourages open dialogue, essential for resolving conflicts and making informed decisions.

The impact of communication is evident in conflict resolution. Misunderstandings often lead to conflicts, and poor communication can exacerbate them. Addressing conflicts with a focus on clear, empathetic, and active engagement can transform contentious situations into opportunities for growth and understanding. For example, rather than accusing someone of being inconsiderate, expressing how their actions affected you opens the door for a constructive conversation. "I felt hurt when you didn't consult me about the changes" invites dialogue and resolution more effectively than "You never consider my input."

In professional settings, effective communication is a linchpin for success. It facilitates collaboration, innovation, and productivity. Teams that communicate well are better equipped to tackle challenges and achieve shared goals. Clear communication of roles, responsibilities, and expectations prevents misunderstandings and ensures everyone is aligned. Moreover, providing constructive feedback and openly discussing ideas fosters an environment where creativity and critical thinking thrive.

Public speaking, a vital aspect of communication, often instills fear in many. However, mastering this skill can significantly enhance personal and professional influence. Effective public speaking involves not only conveying information but also engaging and inspiring the audience. Techniques such as storytelling, using visual aids, and varying vocal tones can capture the audience's attention and make the message more memorable. Practicing public speaking builds confidence, enabling individuals to present their ideas convincingly and persuasively.

Non-verbal communication—body language, facial expressions, and gestures—also plays a crucial role in conveying messages. Often, non-verbal cues can reinforce or contradict what is being said. For instance, a person may say they are fine, but their slouched posture and lack of eye contact might suggest otherwise. Being aware of and controlling non-verbal signals can enhance the clarity and sincerity of the message. Similarly, interpreting others' non-verbal cues can provide additional insights into their true feelings and intentions.

In the digital age, communication extends beyond face-to-face interactions. Emails, texts, and social media have become predominant forms of communication. While these platforms offer convenience and speed, they also present challenges. The absence of tone and body language can lead to misinterpretations. Crafting clear and concise messages, avoiding ambiguous language, and using appropriate emojis or punctuation can mitigate these issues. Additionally, being mindful of digital etiquette—such as responding promptly and respecting privacy—maintains professionalism and respect.

The power of storytelling in communication cannot be overstated. Stories captivate, inspire, and persuade by creating emotional connections. Whether in a personal anecdote shared with friends or a compelling narrative in a business presentation, storytelling makes the message relatable and memorable. A well-told story can illustrate a point more effectively than a list of facts and figures. It humanizes the communicator, making them more approachable and their message more impactful.

Feedback, both giving and receiving, is an essential component of effective communication. Constructive feedback promotes growth and improvement, while positive feedback reinforces good practices and behaviors. When giving feedback, focusing on specific behaviors rather than personal attributes ensures it is received as intended. For instance, "I appreciate how you handled the client's concerns" is more constructive than "You're good with clients." When receiving feedback, approaching it with an open mind and a willingness to improve can transform it into a valuable learning experience.

Communication also serves as a tool for building and maintaining relationships. Expressing appreciation, sharing experiences, and being present in conversations strengthen bonds. Simple acts like saying "thank you," offering compliments, or actively listening during conversations demonstrate respect and value for the other person. These small gestures accumulate over time, building a foundation of trust and mutual respect.

Moreover, setting boundaries through communication is crucial for maintaining healthy relationships. Boundaries define what is acceptable and what is not, helping to protect emotional well-being. Communicating boundaries clearly and respectfully prevents misunderstandings and resentment. For instance, expressing the need for personal space or time to recharge ensures both parties understand and respect each other's needs.

Empathy, active listening, and clarity are not just skills but mindsets that enhance communication. They require continuous practice and self-awareness. Reflecting on past interactions, seeking feedback, and being open to learning new techniques can help improve these skills over time. The journey to becoming an effective communicator is ongoing, but the rewards—stronger relationships, resolved conflicts, and successful collaborations—are well worth the effort.

In essence, communication is the thread that connects us, enabling us to share our thoughts, emotions, and experiences. It is the tool through which we build relationships, solve problems, and achieve our goals. By honing communication skills, we can navigate the complexities of human interaction, fostering understanding, cooperation, and connection. The power of communication lies not just in the words we use but in the empathy, clarity, and active engagement we bring to every interaction. Effective communication also plays a critical role in fostering inclusivity and diversity. In today's interconnected world, people from different cultural, social, and professional backgrounds interact regularly. Understanding and respecting these differences through mindful communication is essential to creating an inclusive environment. This involves being aware of cultural nuances, avoiding stereotypes, and being open to different perspectives. For example, recognizing that direct eye contact might be interpreted differently in various cultures can help avoid misunderstandings and foster mutual respect.

The Journey Ahead: What to Expect

Embarking on any new journey can be both exciting and daunting. The path ahead is often filled with uncertainties and challenges, but it is also rife with opportunities for growth, learning, and transformation. Understanding what to expect and preparing for various scenarios can greatly enhance your ability to navigate this journey successfully. Whether you're starting a new career, launching a business, or setting out on a personal development quest, having a roadmap can make the process more manageable and rewarding.

One of the first things to anticipate on your journey is the initial learning curve. Whenever you start something new, there is a period of adjustment where everything feels unfamiliar and possibly overwhelming. This is perfectly normal. Embrace this phase as an opportunity to absorb as much information as possible. Be curious and ask questions. Seek out mentors or join communities related to your field of interest. Remember, every expert was once a beginner. The knowledge and experience you gain during this initial phase will lay a solid foundation for your future endeavors.

Expect to face obstacles along the way. Challenges are an inevitable part of any journey, but they are also where the most significant growth occurs. Instead of viewing obstacles as setbacks, see them as opportunities to develop resilience and problem-solving skills. When faced with a challenge, take a step back and assess the situation objectively. Break down the problem into smaller, more manageable parts, and tackle them one at a time. Persistence and adaptability are key. The ability to adjust your approach when things don't go as planned will serve you well in the long run.

Another aspect to anticipate is the need for continuous learning and skill development. The world is constantly evolving, and staying relevant requires a commitment to lifelong learning. This might mean taking courses, attending workshops, reading extensively, or learning from peers and mentors. Investing in your education and skill set not only enhances your capabilities but also boosts your confidence. As you advance on your journey, the knowledge and skills you acquire will enable you to tackle more complex challenges and seize new opportunities.

Building a strong support network is crucial. Surround yourself with people who inspire, motivate, and support you. This network can include mentors, peers, friends, and family. Having a support system provides emotional encouragement, practical advice, and sometimes even constructive criticism that can help you grow. Don't hesitate to reach out for help or guidance when needed. Collaboration and networking can open doors to opportunities that you might not have discovered on your own. Furthermore, supporting others in their journeys can create a reciprocal relationship that benefits everyone involved.

Expect moments of self-doubt and uncertainty. It's natural to question your abilities and decisions at times, especially when faced with setbacks or slow progress. During these moments, it's important to remind yourself of your goals and the reasons why you embarked on this journey in the first place. Reflect on your achievements, no matter how small, and use them as motivation to keep moving forward. Developing a positive mindset and practicing self-compassion can help you navigate through periods of doubt.

Setting clear, achievable goals is another essential part of the journey. Goals provide direction and a sense of purpose. Break your larger goals into smaller, actionable steps. This not only makes them more attainable but also allows you to track your progress and celebrate small victories along the way. Regularly review and adjust your goals as needed to stay aligned with your evolving aspirations and circumstances. Goal setting is a dynamic process, and being flexible in your approach can help you stay motivated and focused.

Time management is a skill you'll need to master. Balancing various responsibilities and tasks requires effective time management techniques. Prioritize your tasks based on their importance and deadlines. Use tools like calendars, to-do lists, and time-tracking apps to stay organized. Allocate specific time blocks for focused work, and avoid multitasking as it can reduce productivity. Taking breaks and ensuring you have time for rest and relaxation is also important to maintain your overall well-being and prevent burnout.

Financial planning is another critical aspect, especially if your journey involves starting a business or significant personal investments. Create a realistic budget and track your expenses. Be mindful of your spending and look for ways to save and invest wisely. Understanding basic financial principles and seeking advice from financial experts can help you make informed decisions and avoid common pitfalls. Financial stability provides the peace of mind needed to focus on your goals without unnecessary stress.

Embrace the unpredictability of the journey. While planning and preparation are essential, it's important to remain open to unexpected opportunities and changes. Sometimes, the most rewarding experiences come from unplanned detours. Being flexible and adaptable allows you to take advantage of new paths that align with your goals and values. Embracing uncertainty with a positive attitude can lead to personal growth and new discoveries.

Celebrate your achievements, no matter how small. Recognizing and celebrating your progress is crucial for maintaining motivation and a positive outlook. Take time to reflect on what you have accomplished and express gratitude for the journey itself. Each milestone reached is a testament to your hard work, dedication, and resilience. Celebrations can be simple, like treating yourself to something you enjoy or sharing your success with loved ones. Acknowledging your achievements reinforces your commitment to your goals and fuels your drive to continue.

The journey ahead will undoubtedly be filled with highs and lows, but each experience contributes to your growth and development. By anticipating challenges, continuously learning, building a support network, managing your time and finances, and embracing unpredictability, you can navigate your path with confidence and purpose. Remember, the journey is just as important as the destination. Every step you take, whether forward or backward, is a valuable part of your story. Enjoy the process, learn from every experience, and stay committed to your vision. Maintaining a healthy work-life balance is another crucial element of your journey. While it's important to be dedicated and passionate about your goals, it's equally essential to take care of your personal life and well-being. Overworking can lead to burnout, stress, and a decline in overall health, which ultimately hinders your progress. Set boundaries to ensure you have time for relaxation, hobbies, and spending time with loved ones. Regular exercise, a balanced diet, and sufficient sleep are fundamental to keeping your energy levels high and your mind clear. Remember that taking care of yourself is not a luxury but a necessity for sustained success and happiness.

Chapter 2

Understanding Communication in Relationships

The Basics of Effective Communication

Effective communication is the cornerstone of successful relationships, whether personal or professional. It goes beyond merely exchanging information; it's about understanding the emotions and intentions behind the information. Mastering the basics of effective communication can significantly enhance your interactions, leading to more productive and meaningful exchanges.

Central to effective communication is active listening. Active listening involves fully concentrating, understanding, responding, and then remembering what is being said. It requires more than just hearing words; it involves paying attention to the speaker's body language, tone of voice, and emotional undertones. When you listen actively, you show respect and empathy, making the speaker feel valued and understood. To practice active listening, maintain eye contact, nod in acknowledgment, and avoid interrupting. Reflect back what you've heard by summarizing or paraphrasing to ensure you've grasped the message correctly. This not only clarifies the communication but also demonstrates your engagement in the conversation.

Clear and concise expression is another fundamental aspect of effective communication. Being able to articulate your thoughts and ideas clearly helps prevent misunderstandings and ensures that your message is received as intended. Use simple, straightforward language and avoid jargon that might confuse the listener. Organize your thoughts before speaking, and stay on topic to maintain coherence. Be mindful of your tone, as it can significantly influence how your message is perceived. A calm and positive tone can foster a more open and receptive environment, while a harsh or aggressive tone can create defensiveness and conflict.

Nonverbal communication plays a crucial role in conveying your message. Your body language, facial expressions, gestures, and posture all communicate volumes about your feelings and intentions. Positive body language, such as maintaining eye contact, smiling, and using open gestures, can reinforce your verbal message and build trust. Conversely, negative body language, like crossing your arms, avoiding eye contact, or fidgeting, can undermine your words and create barriers. Being aware of your nonverbal cues and interpreting others' body language can enhance your overall communication effectiveness.

Empathy is essential for connecting with others on a deeper level. It involves understanding and sharing the feelings of another person, which helps build rapport and trust. When you communicate with empathy, you show that you genuinely care about the other person's perspective and emotions. Practice empathy by actively listening, acknowledging the speaker's feelings, and responding with compassion.

Even if you don't agree with their viewpoint, showing empathy can lead to more constructive and respectful dialogues.

Feedback is a vital component of effective communication, especially in a professional setting. Providing constructive feedback helps individuals understand how they can improve and grow. When giving feedback, be specific, focus on behaviors rather than personal attributes, and offer actionable suggestions. Use the "sandwich" approach: start with a positive comment, followed by constructive criticism, and end with another positive remark. This method helps soften the impact of criticism and encourages a positive response. Equally important is being open to receiving feedback. Accepting feedback graciously and using it to improve your skills demonstrates a commitment to personal and professional development.

Cultural awareness is increasingly important in today's globalized world. Different cultures have varied communication styles, norms, and expectations. Being aware of these differences and adapting your communication style accordingly can prevent misunderstandings and foster more effective interactions. For instance, some cultures value direct communication, while others prefer a more indirect approach. Understanding these nuances can help you navigate cross-cultural communications more effectively. Take the time to learn about the cultural backgrounds of the people you interact with and be respectful of their communication preferences.

Conflict resolution is an inevitable part of communication. Disagreements and conflicts arise in any relationship, but how you handle them can make a significant difference. Effective communication involves addressing conflicts calmly and constructively. Focus on the issue at hand rather than personal attacks, and strive to understand the other person's perspective. Use "I" statements to express your feelings and needs without blaming or accusing the other person. For example, say "I feel frustrated when deadlines are missed" instead of "You always miss deadlines." This approach reduces defensiveness and opens the door to collaborative problem-solving.

Building trust through communication is essential for strong relationships. Trust is built over time through consistent, honest, and transparent communication. Be reliable and follow through on your commitments. Share information openly and be willing to admit mistakes and take responsibility for them. Trust is a two-way street; demonstrating trust in others encourages them to trust you in return. Transparent communication fosters a safe environment where people feel comfortable expressing their thoughts and concerns.

Adaptability is another key element of effective communication. Different situations and individuals require different communication styles. Being adaptable means being able to adjust your approach based on the context and the needs of your audience. For instance, the way you communicate with a close friend will differ from how you interact with a colleague or a client. Pay attention to verbal and nonverbal cues from your audience and be willing to modify your style to ensure your message is received effectively.

Emotional intelligence (EI) is crucial for understanding and managing your own emotions, as well as recognizing and influencing the emotions of others. High EI contributes to better communication by helping you navigate social complexities, manage stress, and resolve conflicts. Develop emotional intelligence by practicing self-awareness, self-regulation, motivation, empathy, and social skills. Being emotionally intelligent allows you to communicate more effectively, build stronger relationships, and achieve your goals more efficiently.

Incorporating storytelling into your communication can make your message more engaging and memorable. Stories have the power to connect with people on an emotional level and illustrate your points in a relatable way. Use anecdotes and real-life examples to support your message and capture your audience's attention. A well-told story can make complex information more accessible and inspire action.

Finally, patience and persistence are essential qualities for effective communication. Building strong communication skills takes time and practice. Be patient with yourself and others as you work on improving your abilities. Persistent effort and a commitment to learning will yield positive results over time. Remember that communication is a dynamic process that involves continuous learning and adaptation.

Effective communication is a multifaceted skill that requires intentional practice and mindfulness. By actively listening, expressing yourself clearly, being aware of nonverbal cues, showing empathy, providing and receiving feedback, understanding cultural differences, resolving conflicts constructively, building trust, adapting your style, developing emotional intelligence, using storytelling, and practicing patience and persistence, you can enhance your communication skills and build stronger, more meaningful relationships. Whether in personal interactions or professional environments, mastering these basics will help you navigate your journey with greater ease and success. Effective communication is not a static skill but a dynamic, evolving practice that can continually be refined and improved. As you integrate these foundational elements into your daily interactions, you'll likely notice a significant enhancement in the quality and effectiveness of your communications.

The Role of Emotions in Communication

Emotions permeate every facet of communication, subtly influencing the words we choose, the tone we employ, and the manner in which we convey our messages. Understanding the role of emotions in communication is crucial for cultivating meaningful and effective interactions. Emotions can either facilitate connection and understanding or lead to misunderstanding and conflict, depending on how they are managed and expressed.

Imagine a scenario where you need to deliver constructive feedback to a colleague. If you approach the conversation in a state of irritation, your words may come across as harsh, regardless of your intentions. Conversely, if you approach the same conversation with empathy and calmness, your feedback is more likely to be received positively. This example underscores how emotions can shape the outcome of our interactions.

Emotional awareness is the first step towards harnessing the power of emotions in communication. Being aware of your own emotions and recognizing the emotions of others can help you navigate conversations more effectively. Self-awareness involves understanding your emotional triggers and how they impact your communication style. For instance, if you know that you become defensive when criticized, you can prepare strategies to remain calm and open-minded when receiving feedback.

Similarly, empathy, the ability to understand and share the feelings of another, is pivotal in communication. When you empathize with someone, you are better equipped to respond to their needs and concerns. Empathy fosters trust and connection, making it easier to resolve conflicts and collaborate effectively. To practice empathy, actively listen to the speaker, acknowledge their emotions, and validate their feelings without judgment.

Nonverbal communication is a powerful conduit for emotions. Facial expressions, gestures, posture, and eye contact all convey emotional states. For instance, a genuine smile can express warmth and openness, while crossed arms might indicate defensiveness or discomfort. Being attuned to these nonverbal cues in yourself and others can enhance your ability to communicate effectively. For example, maintaining eye contact shows attentiveness and respect, while nodding can signal agreement and encouragement.

Tone of voice is another critical element that conveys emotions in communication. The same phrase can have different meanings depending on the tone used. A soft, calm tone can soothe and reassure, while a sharp, loud tone can provoke and upset. Being mindful of your tone and adjusting it to suit the context can help you convey your message more effectively. For instance, using a gentle tone when discussing sensitive issues can create a more supportive environment.

Managing emotions is essential for effective communication, especially in high-stakes or emotionally charged situations. Techniques such as deep breathing, mindfulness, and pausing before responding can help you regulate your emotions and respond more thoughtfully. For example, taking a moment to breathe deeply before replying to a provocative comment can prevent an impulsive reaction and allow you to respond more constructively.

Emotions also play a crucial role in persuasion and influence. Appealing to emotions can make your message more compelling and memorable. Storytelling is a powerful way to evoke emotions and connect with your audience. By sharing personal experiences or anecdotes, you can illustrate your points in a relatable and engaging manner. For instance, a leader who shares a story about overcoming a challenge can inspire and motivate their team.

However, it's important to strike a balance between emotional appeal and logical reasoning. While emotions can enhance your message, relying solely on emotional appeal can undermine your credibility. Combining emotional appeal with factual evidence and logical arguments creates a more persuasive and well-rounded message. For example, when presenting a new initiative, complementing data and statistics with stories of potential positive impact can make a stronger case.

Conflict resolution often hinges on managing emotions effectively. When emotions run high, misunderstandings and miscommunications are more likely to occur. Addressing conflicts with emotional intelligence involves recognizing and validating the emotions of all parties involved, while also expressing your own emotions constructively. For instance, using "I" statements to express your feelings, such as "I feel frustrated when deadlines are missed," helps to communicate your emotions without blaming or accusing the other person.

Building emotional resilience is also important for effective communication. Emotional resilience involves the ability to bounce back from setbacks and maintain a positive outlook. This quality can help you navigate difficult conversations and maintain constructive relationships even in challenging circumstances. Techniques such as positive self-talk, reframing negative thoughts, and seeking support from others can strengthen your emotional resilience.

In professional settings, emotional intelligence is particularly valuable. Leaders with high emotional intelligence can inspire and motivate their teams, foster a positive work environment, and navigate organizational dynamics more effectively. For example, a manager who recognizes and addresses team members' emotions can build stronger relationships and enhance team cohesion. Similarly, team members who communicate with empathy and respect can contribute to a more collaborative and productive workplace.

Developing emotional intelligence involves cultivating self-awareness, self-regulation, motivation, empathy, and social skills. Self-awareness is the foundation of emotional intelligence, as it enables you to recognize and understand your own emotions. Self-regulation involves managing your emotions and behaviors in a healthy and constructive manner. Motivation refers to the drive to achieve goals and maintain a positive attitude. Empathy, as mentioned earlier, involves understanding and sharing the feelings of others. Social skills encompass the ability to build and maintain healthy relationships through effective communication and collaboration.

To enhance your emotional intelligence, practice mindfulness and reflection. Mindfulness involves being present in the moment and observing your thoughts and emotions without judgment. Reflection involves reviewing your interactions and considering how your emotions influenced your communication. For example, after a challenging conversation, take a moment to reflect on what emotions you experienced, how they affected your communication, and what you could do differently in the future.

Building strong relationships through communication requires an ongoing commitment to understanding and managing emotions. Whether in personal or professional contexts, the ability to communicate with emotional intelligence can lead to more meaningful and effective interactions. By being aware of your own emotions, empathizing with others, managing your tone and nonverbal cues, and practicing emotional resilience, you can enhance your communication skills and build stronger, more fulfilling relationships.

In summary, emotions are integral to communication, shaping the way we express and interpret messages. Developing emotional awareness and intelligence, practicing empathy, managing emotions constructively, and balancing emotional appeal with logical reasoning are key to effective communication. By mastering these skills, you can navigate conversations with greater ease and build stronger, more meaningful connections with others. Understanding the nuances of emotions in communication can also aid in developing deeper connections and fostering a more supportive environment, both personally and professionally. When we are attuned to the emotional undertones of conversations, we can respond with greater sensitivity and insight, enhancing mutual understanding and collaboration.

Barriers to Effective Communication

Effective communication is often hailed as the cornerstone of successful relationships, both personal and professional. However, numerous barriers can impede the clear exchange of ideas and information, leading to misunderstandings, frustration, and conflict. Recognizing and addressing these barriers is essential for fostering meaningful and productive interactions.

One of the most common barriers to effective communication is physical distance. In an increasingly globalized world, people frequently communicate across vast geographical distances. While technology has made it easier to connect, it also introduces challenges. For example, time zone differences can make it difficult to find mutually convenient times for conversations. Additionally, poor internet connections and technical glitches during virtual meetings can disrupt the flow of communication and lead to misunderstandings.

Language barriers also pose significant challenges. Miscommunication can easily occur when individuals speak different native languages or have varying levels of proficiency in a common language. Even among speakers of the same language, regional accents, dialects, and colloquialisms can complicate understanding. For instance, a phrase that is commonplace in one region might be unfamiliar or even offensive in another. To mitigate these issues, it is crucial to use clear, simple language and to seek clarification when necessary.

Cultural differences further complicate communication. Cultures shape the way people perceive and express themselves, influencing everything from body language to conversational norms. For example, in some cultures, direct eye contact is a sign of confidence and honesty, while in others, it might be perceived as confrontational or disrespectful. Understanding and respecting these cultural nuances can help bridge communication gaps and foster more effective interactions.

Emotional barriers often undermine communication. When individuals are experiencing strong emotions such as anger, fear, or sadness, their ability to communicate clearly and listen effectively can be compromised. Emotional states can color perceptions and lead to misinterpretations of messages. For example, a person who is feeling defensive might interpret a neutral comment as a criticism. Developing emotional intelligence and learning to manage emotions can help individuals communicate more effectively, even in stressful situations.

Psychological barriers, such as biases and prejudices, also hinder effective communication. These mental filters shape how we perceive and interpret information, often leading to distorted understanding. For instance, confirmation bias can cause individuals to favor information that supports their existing beliefs and dismiss information that contradicts them. Overcoming psychological barriers requires self-awareness and a willingness to challenge one's own assumptions and open-mindedly consider different perspectives.

Perceptual barriers arise from differences in how people perceive and interpret the world around them. These differences can be influenced by various factors, including past experiences, education, and personal values. For example, two people might witness the same event but interpret it differently based on their individual backgrounds and beliefs. To overcome perceptual barriers, it is important to practice active listening and strive to understand the other person's point of view.

Environmental barriers, such as noise and distractions, can also impede effective communication. A noisy environment can make it difficult to hear and focus on the conversation, leading to misunderstandings. Similarly, distractions such as multitasking or interruptions can break the flow of communication and cause important details to be missed. Creating a conducive environment for communication, free from unnecessary noise and interruptions, can help ensure that messages are conveyed and received accurately.

Organizational barriers are particularly relevant in professional settings. Hierarchical structures, rigid communication channels, and organizational silos can all obstruct the free flow of information. For example, employees might feel hesitant to speak openly in a highly hierarchical organization where communication is predominantly top-down. Encouraging open communication, flattening organizational structures, and fostering a culture of transparency can help mitigate these barriers and promote more effective communication.

Linguistic barriers, including jargon and technical language, can also impede understanding. In specialized fields, professionals often use terminology that is unfamiliar to those outside the field. While this specialized language can be efficient within the field, it can create confusion when communicating with a broader audience. For instance, a doctor explaining a medical condition to a patient should avoid medical jargon and instead use simple, clear language that the patient can easily understand.

Personal barriers, such as low self-esteem and lack of confidence, can also hinder effective communication. Individuals who doubt their communication abilities might avoid speaking up or expressing their ideas, leading to a lack of participation and missed opportunities for valuable input. Building self-confidence through practice, feedback, and positive reinforcement can help individuals overcome these personal barriers and communicate more effectively.

To address these barriers, it is crucial to develop and practice effective communication skills. Active listening is one of the most important skills for overcoming communication barriers. This involves fully focusing on the speaker, understanding their message, and responding thoughtfully. Techniques such as paraphrasing, summarizing, and asking clarifying questions can help ensure that the message is accurately understood and that the speaker feels heard and valued.

Nonverbal communication also plays a critical role in overcoming barriers. Paying attention to body language, facial expressions, and other nonverbal cues can provide additional context and help clarify the message. For example, maintaining eye contact and nodding can signal attentiveness and agreement, while open body posture can convey openness and receptiveness.

Feedback is another essential component of effective communication. Providing and receiving feedback helps to identify and address misunderstandings, clarify expectations, and improve communication practices. Constructive feedback should be specific, objective, and delivered in a supportive manner. For example, instead of saying, "You never listen to me," a more constructive approach would be, "I feel unheard when I'm interrupted during our conversations."

Building a culture of open communication and trust is also vital for overcoming barriers. Encouraging open dialogue, valuing diverse perspectives, and creating safe spaces for honest communication can help individuals feel more comfortable sharing their thoughts and ideas. For instance, regular team meetings where everyone is encouraged to contribute can foster a more inclusive and collaborative environment.

In summary, barriers to effective communication are numerous and varied, but they can be addressed through awareness, skill development, and intentional efforts to create conducive communication environments. By recognizing and addressing physical, language, cultural, emotional, psychological, perceptual, environmental, organizational, linguistic, and personal barriers, individuals and organizations can enhance their communication effectiveness and build stronger, more meaningful connections. Developing key communication skills, such as active listening, nonverbal communication, and feedback, and fostering a culture of open communication and trust are critical steps in overcoming these barriers and achieving successful communication. Improving communication is an ongoing process that requires commitment and practice. In addition to addressing specific barriers, it is helpful to cultivate a few general habits that support effective communication.

The Impact of Technology on Communication

Technology has revolutionized the way we communicate, transforming both personal interactions and professional exchanges. From the invention of the telephone to the rise of social media, each technological advancement has brought profound changes to our communication landscape. This chapter delves into the multifaceted impact of technology on communication, exploring both the benefits and the challenges it presents.

The advent of the internet marked a significant turning point in communication. Email, one of the earliest forms of internet communication, allowed people to send messages instantly across the globe. This was a stark contrast to traditional mail, which could take days or weeks to deliver. Email enhanced productivity in the workplace by enabling quick exchanges of information and documents, fostering faster decision-making processes.

Social media platforms further altered the communication landscape by offering new ways to connect and share information. Sites like Facebook, Twitter, and Instagram have made it possible for people to stay in touch with friends and family, regardless of geographic distance. These platforms also provide a space for sharing personal milestones, opinions, and content, creating a sense of community and connection.

Instant messaging apps, such as WhatsApp and Messenger, have become integral to daily communication. These apps offer real-time text, voice, and video communication, making it easier to maintain relationships and collaborate with colleagues. Group chat features facilitate team coordination and social interactions within families and friend groups, fostering a sense of inclusivity and immediacy.

Video conferencing technology has transformed professional communication, particularly in the wake of the COVID-19 pandemic. Platforms like Zoom, Microsoft Teams, and Google Meet have enabled remote work and virtual meetings, ensuring business continuity despite physical distancing measures. Video conferencing has also allowed for more flexible work arrangements, such as telecommuting and hybrid work models, which have become increasingly popular.

While technology has undoubtedly enhanced communication, it has also introduced several challenges. One significant issue is the potential for information overload. The constant influx of emails, messages, and notifications can be overwhelming, making it difficult to manage communication effectively. This can lead to stress and decreased productivity, as individuals struggle to keep up with the barrage of information.

Additionally, the reliance on digital communication can sometimes lead to a loss of personal connection.

Text-based communication lacks the nonverbal cues, such as tone of voice and body language, that are crucial for conveying emotions and intentions. This can result in misunderstandings and misinterpretations, as the recipient may not fully grasp the context or sentiment behind the message.

The rise of social media has also given birth to the phenomenon of digital echo chambers. Algorithms on these platforms often curate content based on user preferences and interactions, creating a feedback loop where individuals are exposed primarily to information that aligns with their existing beliefs. This can reinforce biases and limit exposure to diverse perspectives, ultimately hindering meaningful dialogue and understanding.

Privacy and security concerns are another critical aspect of technology's impact on communication. The vast amount of personal information shared online can be vulnerable to data breaches and cyber-attacks. For example, high-profile incidents like the Cambridge Analytica scandal have highlighted the risks associated with data privacy on social media platforms. Ensuring secure communication and protecting sensitive information has become a paramount concern in the digital age.

Despite these challenges, technology continues to drive innovation in communication. Artificial intelligence (AI) and machine learning are being integrated into communication tools to enhance efficiency and personalization. AI-powered chatbots, for instance, can handle customer inquiries and support tasks, providing immediate responses and freeing up human agents for more complex issues.

Language translation tools powered by AI are also breaking down language barriers, enabling seamless communication between speakers of different languages.

Augmented reality (AR) and virtual reality (VR) are emerging technologies that hold promise for transforming communication. AR overlays digital information onto the physical world, enhancing real-time interactions with contextual data. For example, AR can be used in customer service to provide visual instructions for product assembly. VR, on the other hand, creates immersive virtual environments, allowing for more engaging and interactive experiences. In education, VR can simulate real-world scenarios for training purposes, enhancing learning outcomes.

Blockchain technology is another innovation that has the potential to impact communication. By providing a decentralized and secure way to record and verify transactions, blockchain can enhance the transparency and integrity of information. This can be particularly valuable in fields such as journalism, where ensuring the authenticity of information is crucial.

The evolution of communication technology has also led to the rise of remote work and digital nomadism. Remote work allows individuals to work from anywhere with an internet connection, offering greater flexibility and work-life balance. Digital nomads, who leverage technology to work while traveling, epitomize this trend. However, remote work also presents challenges, such as maintaining team cohesion and managing work-life boundaries.

Effective communication tools and strategies are essential for addressing these challenges and ensuring successful remote work arrangements.

In the realm of education, technology has transformed the way we learn and teach. Online learning platforms, such as Coursera and Khan Academy, provide access to a wealth of educational resources and courses from top universities and institutions. Virtual classrooms and learning management systems facilitate communication between students and educators, enabling collaborative learning and real-time feedback. However, the digital divide remains a significant issue, as not all students have equal access to technology and the internet, which can exacerbate educational inequalities.

Healthcare communication has also been revolutionized by technology. Telemedicine allows patients to consult with healthcare providers remotely, increasing access to medical care, especially in underserved areas. Electronic health records (EHRs) streamline the sharing of patient information among healthcare providers, improving the coordination and quality of care. Wearable health devices, such as fitness trackers and smartwatches, enable continuous monitoring of health metrics, providing valuable data for both patients and providers.

As technology continues to advance, it is crucial to strike a balance between leveraging its benefits and mitigating its drawbacks. Developing digital literacy skills is essential for navigating the complexities of modern communication. This includes understanding how to use various communication tools effectively, recognizing the implications of sharing personal information online, and critically evaluating the information encountered on digital platforms.

Promoting digital well-being is also important for maintaining healthy communication habits. This involves setting boundaries to prevent information overload, taking breaks from screens, and fostering face-to-face interactions when possible. Encouraging a mindful approach to technology use can help individuals and organizations reap the benefits of digital communication while minimizing its negative impacts.

In conclusion, technology has undeniably transformed communication, offering numerous benefits such as increased connectivity, efficiency, and access to information. However, it also presents challenges, including information overload, loss of personal connection, and privacy concerns. By understanding and addressing these challenges, and by developing digital literacy and well-being practices, we can harness the power of technology to enhance our communication and build stronger, more meaningful connections. As we continue to navigate the evolving digital landscape, it is essential to remain adaptable and proactive in our approach to communication, ensuring that technology serves as a tool for positive and effective interactions. Embracing the dynamic nature of technological advancements, it becomes increasingly vital to stay current with new developments and trends. This proactive approach allows individuals and organizations to leverage the latest tools and strategies to enhance communication further. For example, the rise of 5G technology promises to revolutionize mobile communication by providing faster internet speeds and more reliable connections, enabling smoother video calls and more efficient data transfer. This can significantly impact remote work, telemedicine, and even everyday social interactions, making them more seamless and integrated.

Case Studies: Communication Success and Failure

Consider the case of a renowned tech company that was once praised for its innovation but later faced a significant communication breakdown that led to a public relations crisis. This company, at its peak, had a robust internal communication system that facilitated seamless collaboration among its teams. Employees were encouraged to share ideas freely, leading to groundbreaking products that significantly impacted the market. However, as the company grew, its communication channels became cluttered, and information silos formed. Critical feedback from lower-level employees failed to reach top executives, resulting in a major product flaw that was not addressed in time. When the product was launched, it received severe backlash from customers, leading to a sharp decline in the company's reputation and stock prices. This case illustrates how poor internal communication can lead to significant failures, even for industry leaders.

Contrast this with the success story of a small startup that managed to disrupt its industry through excellent communication practices. This startup, operating in the highly competitive fintech sector, placed a strong emphasis on transparency and open dialogue from the beginning. The founders held regular all-hands meetings where they shared company goals, challenges, and progress. They implemented a flat organizational structure, ensuring that every employee felt their voice was heard. This approach fostered a culture of trust and collaboration, enabling the team to quickly adapt to market changes and customer feedback. As a result, the startup not only survived but thrived, securing substantial funding and expanding its market share rapidly. Their success underscores the importance of effective communication in fostering innovation and agility.

Another example can be found in the healthcare industry, where communication is crucial for patient safety and care. A leading hospital implemented an advanced electronic health record (EHR) system to streamline communication between doctors, nurses, and other healthcare professionals. This system allowed for real-time updates on patient conditions, reducing the risk of medical errors and improving overall patient outcomes. The hospital also invested in training its staff to use the system effectively, ensuring that everyone was on the same page. Consequently, the hospital saw a significant improvement in patient satisfaction and a reduction in malpractice claims. This case highlights how leveraging technology for effective communication can enhance operational efficiency and service quality.

On the other hand, a well-known multinational corporation faced a major setback due to a failure in external communication. The company launched a global marketing campaign without adequately researching cultural sensitivities in different regions. What was intended to be a humorous advertisement was perceived as offensive in several countries, leading to widespread criticism and boycotts. The company's response was slow and inadequate, further aggravating the situation. It took months of damage control efforts and a significant amount of resources to rebuild its brand image. This example demonstrates the critical importance of understanding and respecting cultural differences in global communication strategies.

Communication failures can also occur in crisis situations, where timely and accurate information is vital. A government agency responsible for disaster management faced criticism for its handling of a major natural disaster. The agency's communication channels were disorganized, resulting in conflicting messages being sent to the public. This confusion exacerbated the panic and hindered rescue efforts. In contrast, another country's disaster management agency had a well-coordinated communication plan in place. They utilized multiple platforms, including social media, to provide clear and consistent updates, ensuring that the public received accurate information promptly. The efficient communication helped manage the crisis effectively, minimizing casualties and damage.

Effective leadership communication is another crucial factor in organizational success. Consider a prominent CEO known for her exceptional communication skills. She regularly engages with employees through town hall meetings, video messages, and an open-door policy. Her transparent and empathetic communication style has built a strong sense of loyalty and motivation among the workforce. This, in turn, has driven the company to achieve remarkable growth and profitability. Conversely, a different company suffered due to its CEO's poor communication. His autocratic style and lack of transparency led to low employee morale and high turnover rates. The company's performance declined as a result, proving that leadership communication directly impacts organizational health and success.

In the realm of customer service, communication plays a pivotal role in shaping customer experience. A popular e-commerce company has set a benchmark with its proactive customer communication. They use personalized emails, chatbots, and social media to keep customers informed about their orders, address queries, and resolve issues swiftly. This approach has earned them a loyal customer base and high satisfaction ratings. Conversely, a telecom company faced massive customer churn due to its poor communication practices. Long wait times, unresponsive support, and vague information frustrated customers, leading them to switch to competitors. This case emphasizes the need for clear, responsive, and customer-centric communication in retaining and satisfying customers.

Team dynamics and project success are also heavily influenced by communication. A software development team working on a critical project for a financial institution demonstrated the importance of regular and structured communication. They adopted agile methodologies, holding daily stand-up meetings and regular sprint reviews. This ensured that everyone was aligned, progress was tracked, and potential issues were addressed promptly. The project was delivered on time and exceeded client expectations. In contrast, another team working on a similar project failed due to poor communication. Lack of regular updates, unclear roles, and missed deadlines led to the project's failure, resulting in financial losses and reputational damage for the firm.

Effective communication is equally vital in educational settings. A university that implemented a comprehensive communication platform for students, faculty, and administration saw significant improvements in engagement and performance. The platform facilitated the sharing of resources, announcements, and feedback, creating a cohesive academic environment. Students were better informed and more involved in their learning process. On the other hand, a school that relied on outdated communication methods struggled with low student engagement and high dropout rates. The lack of timely and accessible information hindered students' ability to stay on track with their studies.

In summary, these case studies illustrate the profound impact of communication on various aspects of organizational and personal success. Whether it's internal communication within a company, external communication with customers, crisis communication, or leadership communication, the principles of clarity, consistency, and empathy are universally applicable. Effective communication fosters trust, collaboration, and agility, enabling organizations to navigate challenges and seize opportunities. Conversely, communication failures can lead to misunderstandings, conflicts, and significant setbacks. By learning from these examples, we can appreciate the importance of cultivating strong communication practices in all areas of life and work. The lessons drawn from these case studies extend beyond the corporate and organizational realms and into personal development. Communication skills are integral to building and maintaining relationships, both professional and personal. For instance, consider an individual who excels in networking due to their exceptional communication abilities. This person actively listens, asks insightful questions, and follows up with personalized messages. Their genuine interest and ability to connect with others have opened numerous opportunities for career advancement and collaborations. On the contrary, another individual who struggles with communication finds it challenging to build a professional network. Their lack of engagement and poor follow-up skills result in missed opportunities and stagnation in their career growth.

Chapter 3

Building Empathy and Understanding

What Is Empathy?

Empathy, a fundamental human trait, is the ability to understand and share the feelings of another person. It transcends mere sympathy, which often involves feeling pity for someone, and instead involves placing oneself in another's shoes to truly grasp their emotional state. This profound connection fosters deeper relationships and can significantly enhance communication and collaboration in both personal and professional settings.

Imagine a scenario where a colleague is visibly distressed after receiving critical feedback from a supervisor. A sympathetic response might involve offering a few comforting words or a pat on the back. However, an empathetic response would go further: you might recall a time when you felt similarly criticized, allowing you to genuinely understand their discomfort. You might say, "I remember feeling really discouraged when I received tough feedback on my project last year. It was tough to process, but eventually, it helped me improve. Do you want to talk about what happened?" This approach not only validates their feelings but also opens the door for a meaningful conversation that can help them address their concerns and find a constructive way forward.

Empathy can be broken down into three main types: cognitive, emotional, and compassionate empathy. Cognitive empathy involves understanding how someone else feels and what they might be thinking. Essentially, it's about perspective-taking. For example, a manager who employs cognitive empathy might anticipate how a new policy could cause anxiety among employees and proactively address their concerns. Emotional empathy, on the other hand, involves physically feeling what another person is experiencing. This type of empathy often leads to strong emotional connections and can be particularly powerful in personal relationships. Lastly, compassionate empathy goes a step further by not only understanding and feeling what someone else is going through but also being moved to help them. It's the driving force behind acts of kindness and support.

Developing empathy begins with active listening. When someone speaks, truly listen to them without planning your response while they are talking. Make eye contact, nod in acknowledgment, and avoid interrupting. This type of attentive listening demonstrates that you value their words and are genuinely interested in their perspective. Reflecting back what you've heard can also be beneficial. For instance, you might say, "It sounds like you're really frustrated with the current situation at work. That must be tough to handle." This not only confirms your understanding but also encourages the speaker to delve deeper into their feelings.

Nonverbal communication is another crucial aspect of empathy. Body language, facial expressions, and tone of voice can convey empathy even without words. A warm smile, a reassuring touch on the shoulder, or a gentle tone can all communicate understanding and support. Being mindful of these cues can help you connect more deeply with others and make them feel seen and heard.

Empathy also requires an open mind and a willingness to be vulnerable. It's essential to let go of judgments and preconceived notions about others. This openness allows you to appreciate their unique experiences and perspectives. Being vulnerable, on the other hand, means being comfortable with your own emotions and willing to share them. When you share your feelings and experiences, you invite others to do the same, fostering a deeper emotional connection.

In a professional context, empathy can transform leadership and team dynamics. Leaders who practice empathy often build stronger, more cohesive teams. They understand the individual strengths and challenges of their team members, which allows them to provide tailored support and guidance. For example, an empathetic leader might recognize that an employee is struggling with a heavy workload due to personal issues at home. Instead of reprimanding them for missed deadlines, the leader might offer flexible working hours or additional resources to help them manage their responsibilities. This not only alleviates the employee's stress but also builds loyalty and trust within the team.

Empathy also plays a crucial role in customer service. Consider a customer service representative who receives a call from an irate customer. An empathetic response might involve acknowledging the customer's frustration and expressing a genuine desire to resolve the issue. The representative might say, "I'm really sorry to hear that you've had such a frustrating experience. I understand how that feels, and I'm here to help you find a solution." This response not only addresses the customer's immediate concern but also helps to rebuild trust and improve the overall customer experience.

In education, empathy can significantly enhance the learning environment. Teachers who demonstrate empathy can better understand the individual needs and challenges of their students. For example, a teacher who notices a student struggling with a particular subject might take the time to offer additional support and encouragement, rather than simply marking them down for poor performance. This approach can boost the student's confidence and motivation, leading to improved academic outcomes.

In healthcare, empathy is essential for providing patient-centered care. Medical professionals who show empathy can better understand their patients' concerns and build stronger doctor-patient relationships. For instance, a doctor who listens empathetically to a patient's fears about a diagnosis can provide reassurance and support, which can significantly improve the patient's emotional well-being and adherence to treatment plans.

Empathy is also vital in conflict resolution. When mediating a dispute, understanding the emotions and perspectives of all parties involved is crucial for finding a mutually acceptable solution. An empathetic mediator can acknowledge the feelings of each party, validate their concerns, and facilitate a dialogue that encourages cooperation and compromise. This approach can help to resolve conflicts more effectively and build lasting agreements.

Developing empathy is a continuous process that requires self-awareness and practice. One effective way to cultivate empathy is through mindfulness and reflection. Taking time to reflect on your own emotions and experiences can help you better understand and relate to the emotions of others. Mindfulness practices, such as meditation, can also enhance your ability to stay present and attentive in your interactions with others.

Another way to build empathy is by seeking out diverse experiences and perspectives. Engaging with people from different backgrounds, cultures, and walks of life can broaden your understanding of the world and enhance your ability to empathize with others. Volunteering, traveling, and participating in community activities are all excellent ways to gain new insights and develop a more empathetic outlook.

Empathy is not just an innate trait but a skill that can be nurtured and developed over time. By actively practicing empathy in your daily interactions, you can create more meaningful connections, foster a supportive and inclusive environment, and positively impact the lives of those around you. Whether in personal relationships, professional settings, or broader social contexts, empathy is a powerful tool for building understanding, compassion, and collaboration. Empathy's impact extends far beyond individual relationships and can create ripple effects that influence entire communities and societies. When people feel understood and valued, they are more likely to contribute positively to their communities and engage in behaviors that promote social cohesion. This collective empathy can lead to stronger, more resilient communities that are better equipped to address shared challenges and work towards common goals.

Active Listening Techniques

Active listening is an essential skill that goes beyond merely hearing words; it involves fully engaging with the speaker, understanding their message, and responding thoughtfully. This technique enhances communication, builds stronger relationships, and fosters mutual respect and understanding. Mastering active listening requires practice, patience, and a willingness to be present in the moment.

Imagine you're at a team meeting where a colleague is presenting a new project proposal. Instead of merely nodding along or intermittently checking your phone, active listening means giving your full attention to the speaker. You maintain eye contact, note their key points, and show through your body language that you're engaged. When they finish speaking, you might say, "I see you're really passionate about this new approach. Can you elaborate on how it will impact our current workflow?" This demonstrates that you've not only heard but also processed their message and are interested in learning more.

One of the most fundamental aspects of active listening is maintaining eye contact. This simple yet powerful gesture conveys interest and respect. When you look someone in the eye, it shows that you are fully present and engaged in the conversation. However, it's important to balance eye contact with natural breaks to avoid making the other person uncomfortable. Think of it as a dance—synchronizing your gaze with the flow of the conversation.

Another crucial component is avoiding interruptions. When someone is speaking, it can be tempting to interject with your own thoughts or solutions. However, interrupting can disrupt their train of thought and make them feel unheard. Instead, practice patience by allowing them to finish their points before responding. If you find yourself eager to jump in, take a deep breath and remind yourself that your turn to speak will come. This patience not only shows respect but also ensures you fully understand their message before forming a response.

Reflective listening is a technique where you paraphrase what the speaker has said to confirm your understanding. For example, if a friend shares their frustration about a project, you might respond, "It sounds like you're feeling overwhelmed with the project deadlines and lack of support from the team." This not only validates their feelings but also provides an opportunity for them to clarify or expand on their thoughts. Reflective listening helps ensure there are no misunderstandings and demonstrates that you are genuinely engaged with their experience.

Asking open-ended questions is another powerful tool in active listening. These questions encourage the speaker to elaborate and provide more in-depth responses, fostering a richer conversation. For instance, instead of asking, "Did you have a good day?" you might ask, "What was the highlight of your day?" This invites the speaker to share more detailed and meaningful information, leading to a more engaging dialogue.

Nonverbal communication plays a significant role in active listening. Your body language, facial expressions, and gestures all convey your level of engagement. Nodding occasionally, leaning slightly forward, and maintaining an open posture can all signal that you're actively listening. Conversely, crossing your arms, looking around the room, or checking your watch can indicate disinterest or impatience. Be mindful of these nonverbal cues to ensure they align with your intent to be an active listener.

Silence can be a powerful aspect of active listening. Allowing moments of silence gives the speaker time to think and feel comfortable continuing their thoughts. It also provides you with a moment to process what has been said before responding. Embracing silence can lead to deeper, more thoughtful conversations and shows that you are comfortable with letting the speaker take their time.

Empathy is closely tied to active listening. To truly understand someone's perspective, you must put yourself in their shoes and experience their emotions. When a friend shares a personal struggle, empathetic listening involves not only hearing their words but also feeling their pain and offering genuine support. You might say, "I can't imagine how difficult this must be for you, but I'm here to support you in any way I can." This response shows that you are not only listening but also deeply caring about their well-being.

Summarizing key points at the end of a conversation can reinforce your understanding and show that you've been paying attention. For example, after a lengthy discussion with a colleague about a project, you might conclude with, "To summarize, we've agreed to implement the new strategy starting next month, and I'll take the lead on coordinating the team. Does that sound right?" This helps ensure everyone is on the same page and that no important details have been overlooked.

Providing feedback is another critical aspect of active listening. Constructive feedback should be specific, focused on behaviors rather than personal attributes, and delivered with empathy. For example, instead of saying, "You're always late with your reports," you might say, "I've noticed that the last few reports were submitted past the deadline. Is there something we can do to help you manage the workload better?" This approach addresses the issue without making the person feel attacked and opens the door for a productive conversation.

Active listening also involves being aware of cultural differences that may influence communication styles. Different cultures have varying norms regarding eye contact, silence, gestures, and personal space. Being sensitive to these differences and adjusting your listening approach accordingly can enhance cross-cultural communication and prevent misunderstandings.

Practicing active listening in group settings can be particularly challenging but equally important. In meetings or group discussions, it's crucial to give each speaker your full attention and avoid side conversations or distractions. Summarizing group discussions, asking clarifying questions, and ensuring everyone has the opportunity to speak are all ways to practice active listening in a group context.

Developing active listening skills takes time and practice. It requires a conscious effort to be present, patient, and empathetic in every conversation. Start by setting small goals, such as focusing on maintaining eye contact or practicing reflective listening in your daily interactions. Over time, these practices will become more natural, and you'll find that your communication skills and relationships improve significantly.

Active listening is not just a technique but a mindset. It involves approaching every conversation with the intent to understand and connect with the speaker. By practicing active listening, you can build stronger, more meaningful relationships, enhance your communication skills, and create a more supportive and empathetic environment in both your personal and professional life.

Embrace the power of active listening and watch as it transforms your interactions and deepens your connections with others. Whether in a heartfelt conversation with a loved one or a critical discussion at work, active listening is the key to truly understanding and being understood. To truly master active listening, one must also be aware of internal distractions and biases that can hinder the process. Internal distractions include your own thoughts, emotions, or preconceived notions that may interfere with your ability to fully engage with the speaker. Recognizing when your mind starts to wander and gently bringing your focus back to the conversation is crucial. This mindfulness practice can significantly enhance your listening abilities.

Practicing Empathy in Daily Conversations

Empathy is the ability to understand and share the feelings of another person, a skill that lies at the heart of meaningful human connection. In daily conversations, practicing empathy can transform ordinary interactions into profound exchanges that foster trust, respect, and deeper relationships. It's a skill that can be cultivated through mindful practice and a genuine desire to connect with others on a deeper level.

Imagine you're having a conversation with a coworker who seems unusually quiet and withdrawn. Instead of dismissing their behavior or jumping to conclusions, practicing empathy involves taking a moment to notice these subtle cues and showing genuine concern. You might say, "I've noticed you seem a bit down today. Is everything okay?" This simple act of reaching out demonstrates that you care about their well-being and are willing to listen if they choose to share.

Empathy begins with active listening, which means being fully present in the moment and giving the speaker your undivided attention. This involves not just hearing the words but also paying attention to the speaker's tone, body language, and emotions. For example, if a friend is talking about a recent disappointment, you might notice their slumped posture and subdued voice, indicating they are feeling down. Acknowledging these non-verbal signals by saying, "I can see this really affected you," shows that you are attuned to their emotional state and are offering support.

Another key aspect of empathy is withholding judgment and avoiding the urge to immediately offer solutions or advice. Often, people just want to be heard and understood rather than fixed. When a family member vents about a stressful day at work, instead of jumping in with suggestions on how to manage their stress, simply acknowledging their feelings can be more powerful. You might say, "That sounds incredibly frustrating. It must be tough to deal with so much pressure." This response validates their experience and shows that you are there to support them without trying to take control of the situation.

Sharing your own experiences can also build empathy, but it's important to do so in a way that doesn't overshadow the other person's feelings. If a friend is grieving the loss of a pet, you might share a brief story about your own experience with loss, followed by, "I remember how hard that was for me. I'm here for you if you need to talk." This approach helps to create a shared understanding while keeping the focus on their experience.

Asking open-ended questions is another effective way to practice empathy. These questions encourage the speaker to express themselves more fully and provide insights into their thoughts and feelings. Instead of asking, "Are you okay?" which might elicit a simple yes or no, you could ask, "How are you feeling about everything that's been going on?" This invites the person to share more about their internal experience, giving you a better understanding of their perspective.

Empathy also involves recognizing and respecting cultural differences that may influence how people express emotions and communicate. In some cultures, direct eye contact is a sign of respect and engagement, while in others it might be considered rude or confrontational. Being aware of these differences and adjusting your communication style accordingly can help you connect more effectively with people from diverse backgrounds. This cultural sensitivity enhances empathy by showing that you respect their norms and values.

Practicing empathy can be particularly challenging in situations of conflict, but it is also where it is most needed. During a disagreement, it's easy to become defensive and focus solely on getting your point across. However, taking a step back to understand the other person's perspective can lead to more productive and respectful conversations. For example, if you're in a heated debate with a colleague, you might say, "I can see this issue is very important to you. Can you help me understand why you feel this way?" This approach shows that you value their viewpoint and are willing to consider it, even if you ultimately disagree.

Empathy is not just about understanding others' emotions but also about expressing your own in a way that invites connection. Being open about your feelings can encourage others to do the same, creating a reciprocal dynamic of empathy. For instance, if you're feeling overwhelmed by a project, sharing this with a teammate by saying, "I'm feeling a bit overwhelmed by the deadlines. How are you managing with everything?" can open up a dialogue where both of you can support each other.

In daily conversations, empathy can also be practiced through small acts of kindness and thoughtful gestures. Sending a quick message to check in on a friend you know is going through a tough time, offering to help a neighbor with groceries, or simply giving a genuine compliment can all demonstrate empathy and strengthen your connections with others. These actions show that you are thinking about others and care about their well-being, even in small, everyday ways.

Reflecting on your conversations at the end of the day can help you become more empathetic. Consider moments when you felt truly connected with someone and what contributed to that feeling. Likewise, think about interactions that could have gone better and what you might do differently next time. This self-reflection helps you learn from your experiences and continuously improve your empathetic skills.

Empathy also extends to self-empathy, which involves being kind and understanding towards yourself. Recognizing your own emotions and treating yourself with the same compassion you would offer to others is crucial for maintaining emotional well-being. When you're feeling stressed or overwhelmed, taking a moment to acknowledge your feelings and giving yourself permission to take a break can help you recharge and be more present for others.

In professional settings, empathy can greatly enhance teamwork and collaboration. Leaders who practice empathy can create a more inclusive and supportive work environment, where employees feel valued and understood. For example, a manager who notices an employee struggling with workload might say, "I've noticed you've been putting in a lot of extra hours lately. How are you managing, and is there anything I can do to help?" This shows concern for the employee's well-being and encourages open communication.

Ultimately, empathy is about building a bridge between yourself and others, creating a space where people feel seen, heard, and valued. It requires a conscious effort to step outside of your own perspective and fully engage with another person's experience. By practicing empathy in daily conversations, you can foster deeper connections, enhance your communication skills, and create a more compassionate and understanding world.

Incorporating empathy into your interactions is a journey that involves continuous learning and growth. It's about being present, listening deeply, and responding with kindness and understanding. As you cultivate this skill, you'll find that your relationships become richer and more fulfilling, and you'll contribute to a more empathetic and connected community. Empathy, once integrated into your daily interactions, can transform not only your personal connections but also the broader social dynamics you engage in. Consider the ripple effect of empathetic communication: when you show empathy, it encourages others to do the same, creating a culture of understanding and respect. This is particularly powerful in environments such as workplaces, schools, and community groups, where fostering a sense of belonging can lead to greater cooperation and collective well-being.

Overcoming Judgment and Bias

Judgment and bias are deeply ingrained in human nature, often serving as automatic responses to new information and social interactions. These tendencies can cloud our perceptions, hinder our relationships, and limit our personal growth. Overcoming judgment and bias requires conscious effort, self-awareness, and a commitment to seeing the world through a more open and understanding lens.

Imagine you're at a social gathering, and you meet someone whose opinions starkly contrast with your own. The immediate instinct might be to dismiss their views or label them negatively. However, overcoming judgment starts with recognizing this initial reaction and choosing to engage with curiosity instead of condemnation. You might ask, "What experiences led you to this perspective?" Such a question not only opens a dialogue but also shows respect for the other person's background and beliefs.

The first step in overcoming judgment is cultivating self-awareness. This involves examining your own prejudices and understanding where they come from. Reflect on your upbringing, cultural influences, and personal experiences that have shaped your worldview. For instance, if you find yourself judging someone based on their appearance, consider why you hold these views. Are they based on stereotypes perpetuated by media or past negative encounters? By identifying the roots of your biases, you can begin to challenge and dismantle them.

Another effective strategy is to practice mindfulness. Mindfulness involves being present in the moment and observing your thoughts without immediate reaction. When you notice a judgmental thought arising, instead of acting on it, take a moment to breathe and acknowledge it. Say to yourself, "I'm noticing that I'm making a judgment right now." This simple act of recognition can create a mental space that allows you to choose a more compassionate response.

Engaging with diverse perspectives is crucial in overcoming bias. Seek out opportunities to interact with people from different backgrounds, cultures, and life experiences. This could be through multicultural events, diverse literature, or traveling to new places. For example, attending a cultural festival or reading books by authors from various backgrounds can broaden your understanding and appreciation of different viewpoints. The more you expose yourself to diversity, the more you realize the richness it brings to life.

Empathy plays a significant role in overcoming judgment. Putting yourself in someone else's shoes can transform your perception of them. Consider a scenario where a colleague consistently arrives late to meetings. Instead of labeling them as lazy or irresponsible, try to understand their situation. Perhaps they are dealing with personal challenges, such as caring for a sick family member or managing a long commute. Approaching them with empathy, you might say, "I've noticed you've been late a few times. Is everything okay?" This not only shows concern but also opens a pathway for understanding their circumstances.

Critical thinking is another powerful tool. It involves questioning your assumptions and seeking evidence before forming conclusions. When you catch yourself making a snap judgment, pause and ask, "What facts do I have to support this belief? Is there another explanation?" For example, if you assume someone is unfriendly because they didn't greet you, consider other possibilities, such as them being preoccupied or shy. By challenging your assumptions, you can reduce the influence of bias on your interactions.

Building relationships with individuals who challenge your perspectives can be immensely beneficial. Friendships or collaborations with people who think differently encourage you to see issues from multiple angles. These relationships can be uncomfortable initially, but they foster personal growth and broaden your understanding. For instance, working on a project with someone who has a different approach can teach you new methods and ideas, enhancing your own skills and knowledge.

Education is a lifelong journey that helps in overcoming judgment and bias. Educate yourself about social issues, historical contexts, and psychological principles that contribute to bias. Understanding concepts like confirmation bias, where people favor information that confirms their pre-existing beliefs, can help you recognize and counteract these tendencies in yourself. Additionally, learning about the history and experiences of marginalized groups can deepen your empathy and reduce prejudices.

Humility is essential in overcoming judgment. Accept that you don't have all the answers and that your perspective is just one among many. This attitude allows for continuous learning and growth. When you encounter new information or perspectives, approach them with a mindset of curiosity rather than defensiveness. Ask questions, listen actively, and be willing to revise your beliefs in light of new evidence.

Creating inclusive environments is another crucial aspect. Whether in the workplace, social circles, or community groups, fostering inclusivity helps reduce bias. Encourage open dialogues where everyone feels safe to share their perspectives without fear of judgment. For example, in team meetings, you might ensure that quieter members have the opportunity to speak, thus valuing all voices equally. Inclusivity not only enriches discussions but also builds a culture of respect and understanding.

Accountability is vital in the journey to overcome bias. Hold yourself accountable for your actions and words. When you recognize that you've made a judgmental comment or acted on a bias, take responsibility and make amends. Apologize if necessary and reflect on how you can do better in the future. This accountability reinforces your commitment to fairness and personal growth.

Mentorship can also play a role in overcoming judgment. Seek mentors who exemplify open-mindedness and empathy. Learn from their experiences and ask for guidance on how to navigate your own biases. Conversely, be a mentor to others, sharing your journey and encouraging them to challenge their own prejudices. This reciprocal relationship fosters a community of continuous learning and mutual support.

Lastly, patience is essential. Overcoming judgment and bias is not an overnight transformation but a gradual process. Be patient with yourself and others as you navigate this journey. Celebrate small victories, such as moments when you successfully challenge a bias or respond with empathy instead of judgment. Recognize that setbacks are part of the learning process and use them as opportunities for growth.

Incorporating these practices into your daily life can significantly reduce the impact of judgment and bias on your interactions. It requires a sustained effort and a genuine desire to understand and connect with others. By committing to this path, you not only enhance your relationships but also contribute to a more inclusive and compassionate society.

The journey to overcome judgment and bias is ongoing, but with dedication and mindfulness, it is entirely achievable. Each step you take brings you closer to a more open-hearted and enlightened way of living, where you can fully appreciate the rich tapestry of human experience. Embrace this journey with courage and compassion, knowing that every effort you make contributes to a better world for yourself and those around you. As you continue on this path, it's important to recognize that overcoming judgment and bias is not a solitary endeavor. Building supportive networks can amplify your efforts.

Surround yourself with like-minded individuals who are also committed to personal growth and inclusivity. These communities can provide encouragement, share valuable insights, and hold each other accountable. For instance, joining a book club focused on social justice or participating in workshops on cultural competency can deepen your understanding and commitment.

Exercises for Building Empathy

Empathy is the cornerstone of meaningful human connections, allowing us to understand and share the feelings of others. Building empathy requires intentional practice and a genuine desire to connect with others on a deeper level. Various exercises can help nurture and strengthen this vital skill, transforming how we interact with the world around us.

One effective exercise for building empathy is active listening. This involves fully concentrating, understanding, responding, and then remembering what is being said. It's more than just hearing words; it's about being present and engaged. Suppose a friend is sharing a difficult experience. To practice active listening, you might nod to show understanding, maintain eye contact, and avoid interrupting. Reflect back what they said by summarizing, such as, "It sounds like you're feeling overwhelmed with work and personal commitments." This not only validates their feelings but also shows that you are genuinely invested in their experience.

Another powerful exercise is perspective-taking. This involves imagining yourself in someone else's situation and considering how you would feel and react. For example, if a colleague is upset about a project setback, try to put yourself in their shoes. Ask yourself, "How would I feel if I were facing this challenge?" This mental exercise helps you appreciate their emotions and develop a more compassionate response. You might say, "I can see why this situation is frustrating. Let's brainstorm some solutions together."

Journaling can also be a valuable tool for building empathy. Take time each day to write about your interactions and reflect on how you responded to others' emotions. Consider questions like, "Did I show empathy in that situation?" or "How could I have been more understanding?" By regularly examining your behavior, you can identify areas for improvement and track your progress over time.

Engaging in role-playing scenarios is another effective way to build empathy. This exercise can be done in pairs or groups, where participants take on different roles and act out various situations. For example, one person might play the role of a customer service representative dealing with an irate customer. The goal is to practice responding with empathy and understanding. Afterward, discuss what was challenging and what was successful. Role-playing helps develop the ability to remain calm and compassionate under pressure.

Reading fiction is a surprisingly effective method for enhancing empathy. Studies have shown that immersing yourself in stories and characters can improve your ability to understand others' emotions and perspectives. Choose books that offer diverse viewpoints and complex characters. As you read, pay attention to the characters' feelings, motivations, and challenges. This practice can help you become more attuned to the nuances of human emotions in real life.

Volunteering is another practical way to build empathy. Working with people from different backgrounds and life situations can broaden your understanding and compassion. For instance, volunteering at a homeless shelter can expose you to the struggles faced by those experiencing homelessness. Listening to their stories and offering support fosters a deeper sense of empathy and human connection. It also provides valuable insights into the systemic issues that contribute to their circumstances.

Mindfulness meditation can also enhance empathy by helping you become more aware of your own emotions and those of others. Spend a few minutes each day practicing mindfulness. Focus on your breath and observe your thoughts and feelings without judgment. As you become more in tune with your own emotional landscape, you will find it easier to recognize and understand the emotions of others. This heightened awareness can lead to more empathetic interactions.

Participating in empathy-building workshops or training programs can provide structured opportunities to develop this skill. These programs often include a variety of exercises, such as group discussions, storytelling, and interactive activities designed to enhance empathy. For example, a workshop might involve sharing personal stories and practicing empathetic responses in a safe and supportive environment. These experiences can be transformative, offering new perspectives and techniques for connecting with others.

Practicing gratitude can also foster empathy. Take time each day to reflect on the positive aspects of your life and express appreciation for the people who contribute to your well-being. This practice can shift your focus from your own challenges to the kindness and generosity of others. Expressing gratitude, whether through a thank-you note or a verbal acknowledgment, can strengthen your relationships and enhance your ability to empathize with others' experiences.

Engaging in cultural exchange activities can broaden your understanding and appreciation of different perspectives. Attend cultural events, try new cuisines, or learn about traditions and customs from around the world. These experiences can challenge your assumptions and open your mind to the richness of human diversity. For example, participating in a cultural festival can expose you to different ways of life and foster a greater sense of empathy for people from various backgrounds.

Storytelling is a powerful tool for building empathy. Sharing your own stories and listening to others' can create deep emotional connections. Organize or participate in storytelling events where people can openly share their experiences. As you listen, focus on understanding the emotions behind the stories. This practice can help you develop a deeper appreciation for the complexities of others' lives and enhance your ability to respond with empathy.

Another exercise is practicing self-empathy, which involves being kind and understanding toward yourself. Recognize your own emotions and give yourself permission to feel them without judgment. Treat yourself with the same compassion you would offer a friend. For instance, if you're feeling stressed, acknowledge your feelings and remind yourself that it's okay to take a break. Practicing self-empathy can improve your emotional resilience and make it easier to extend empathy to others.

Engaging in reflective conversations with a trusted friend or mentor can also help build empathy. Discuss your experiences and explore how you responded to others' emotions. Seek feedback on your empathetic skills and ask for suggestions on how to improve. These conversations can provide valuable insights and support your journey toward becoming more empathetic.

Lastly, practicing forgiveness can enhance empathy. Holding onto grudges and resentment can cloud your ability to understand and connect with others. Work on letting go of past hurts and forgiving those who have wronged you. This doesn't mean condoning harmful behavior, but rather freeing yourself from the negative emotions that hinder empathy. Forgiveness can create space for more compassionate and empathetic interactions.

Incorporating these exercises into your daily life can significantly enhance your empathy skills. It requires consistent effort and a genuine desire to connect with others on a deeper level. As you practice these exercises, you'll likely notice a positive shift in your relationships and a greater sense of connection with the world around you. Empathy is a journey, and with dedication, you can make meaningful strides toward becoming a more compassionate and understanding individual. Building empathy is a continuous journey that evolves over time. As you integrate empathy-building exercises into your daily life, you will likely experience profound changes not only in your relationships but also in your overall worldview. The ability to genuinely understand and share the feelings of others enhances your capacity for kindness, patience, and cooperation.

Chapter 4

Communicating Love and Affection

The Five Love Languages

Understanding and expressing love effectively can profoundly impact relationships, making them richer and more fulfilling. The concept of the five love languages, introduced by Dr. Gary Chapman, provides a framework for understanding how people give and receive love. These languages are Words of Affirmation, Acts of Service, Receiving Gifts, Quality Time, and Physical Touch. Each person has a primary love language that resonates most with them, and recognizing these languages in ourselves and others can enhance our relationships.

Words of Affirmation involve expressing love through spoken or written words. Compliments, words of appreciation, and verbal encouragement are powerful tools in this love language. For someone whose primary love language is Words of Affirmation, hearing "I love you," "You mean so much to me," or "I appreciate what you do" can be incredibly meaningful. It's not just about saying nice things; it's about being sincere and specific. For example, instead of a generic "Good job," you might say, "I really appreciate how you handled that project with such attention to detail and creativity." The key is to make the person feel seen and valued for who they are and what they do.

Acts of Service are about showing love through actions rather than words. This love language is all about doing things you know your partner would like. It involves taking on tasks that ease their burden or make their life easier. For instance, preparing a meal, doing the laundry, or running errands can speak volumes to someone who values Acts of Service. These actions demonstrate thoughtfulness and a willingness to go out of your way to make your partner's life better. It's essential to perform these acts without expecting anything in return, as genuine love is the driving force behind them.

Receiving Gifts is a love language where the act of giving and receiving tangible items holds special significance. It's not about materialism but about the thought and effort behind the gift. For those who resonate with this love language, a well-chosen gift can communicate that they are known, cared for, and valued. It could be as simple as bringing home their favorite snack or as elaborate as planning a surprise vacation. The importance lies in the gesture and the emotional connection it represents. Gifts serve as visual symbols of love and reminders of your affection.

Quality Time is about giving someone your undivided attention. This love language emphasizes the importance of being present and engaged with your partner. It involves meaningful conversations, shared activities, and making memories together. For someone who values Quality Time, distractions like smartphones or television can be detrimental. They thrive on one-on-one interactions where they feel heard and understood. Whether it's a quiet evening at home or an adventurous day out, the focus should be on creating a sense of togetherness and connection.

Physical Touch is a powerful love language that involves expressing love through physical contact. For those who prioritize Physical Touch, gestures like holding hands, hugging, kissing, or a gentle touch on the back can convey deep affection. This love language is not solely about sexual intimacy but includes all forms of physical closeness. Physical Touch can provide comfort, security, and a sense of belonging. It's about using touch to communicate warmth and love, making the person feel cherished and connected.

Understanding your own love language and that of your partner can transform your relationship. It allows you to express love in ways that are most meaningful to each other, fostering deeper emotional intimacy. To discover your love language, reflect on what makes you feel most loved and appreciated. Consider how you naturally express love to others, as this can be a clue to your primary love language. Additionally, observing your partner's behavior and listening to their requests can provide insights into their love language.

Once you've identified your love languages, it's important to communicate them to each other. Open and honest discussions about what makes you feel loved can prevent misunderstandings and unmet expectations. For example, if your love language is Acts of Service, you might explain to your partner how much it means to you when they help out with household chores. Conversely, if your partner's love language is Quality Time, you can make an effort to plan regular date nights or unplug from distractions to spend focused time together.

Incorporating the five love languages into your daily life requires intentionality and effort. It's about making a conscious choice to express love in ways that resonate with your partner. For instance, if your partner's love language is Words of Affirmation, make it a habit to compliment them regularly and express gratitude for their efforts. If they value Acts of Service, look for opportunities to help them with tasks, even without being asked. For those who appreciate Receiving Gifts, remember special occasions and surprise them with thoughtful presents. If Quality Time is their love language, prioritize spending uninterrupted time together. For Physical Touch, incorporate more affectionate gestures into your daily interactions.

It's also important to understand that love languages can evolve over time. Life circumstances, personal growth, and changes in the relationship can influence how we give and receive love. Regular check-ins with your partner about each other's love languages can ensure that you continue to meet each other's emotional needs. Flexibility and adaptability in expressing love can help maintain a strong and healthy relationship.

Recognizing and respecting your partner's love language can also prevent conflicts and misunderstandings. For example, if your love language is Receiving Gifts but your partner's is Acts of Service, you might feel unloved if they don't give you gifts frequently. However, understanding that they express love through actions can help you appreciate their efforts and feel more valued. Similarly, if your partner values Quality Time but you prioritize Physical Touch, finding a balance that honors both of your needs can strengthen your bond.

Ultimately, the five love languages provide a practical framework for nurturing and sustaining love in relationships. By learning to speak your partner's love language and teaching them yours, you create a mutual understanding and appreciation that deepens your connection. Love is a dynamic and evolving journey, and the five love languages offer valuable tools to navigate it successfully. Through intentional and thoughtful expressions of love, you can build a relationship that is rich, fulfilling, and enduring.

Understanding and applying the five love languages can revolutionize how you experience and express love. It brings clarity to your emotional needs and those of your partner, fostering a more harmonious and satisfying relationship. As you continue to explore and practice these love languages, you'll find that love becomes not only a feeling but a deliberate and meaningful action. The five love languages are not just theoretical concepts but practical tools that can be applied in everyday life to enhance your relationships. Integrating these love languages into your daily routines can make your connections more vibrant and resilient. Here are some additional insights and strategies to help you deepen your understanding and application of the five love languages.

Verbal Expressions of Love

Verbal expressions of love are a cornerstone of many intimate relationships, serving as a direct and powerful way to communicate affection, appreciation, and commitment. The words we choose, how we say them, and the frequency with which we express them can deeply influence the emotional climate of our relationships. Mastering the art of verbal expressions of love requires understanding the nuances of communication, empathy, and sincerity.

In the early days of a relationship, verbal expressions of love often come easily. Compliments, sweet nothings, and declarations of love flow naturally as two people get to know each other and build their bond. However, as time passes and the initial excitement settles into routine, maintaining this level of verbal expression can require more conscious effort. It's important to recognize that consistent verbal affirmation can strengthen a relationship, while its absence can lead to feelings of neglect and disconnection.

One of the simplest yet most profound ways to express love verbally is through daily affirmations. Telling your partner "I love you" regularly reinforces your emotional connection. However, these words should never become rote or automatic. Each time you say them, ensure they are backed by genuine emotion and presence. Look into your partner's eyes, hold their hand, and let them feel the depth of your affection through your tone and expression.

Beyond the classic "I love you," specific compliments and acknowledgments can have a significant impact.

People thrive on feeling seen and appreciated for who they are and what they do. Complimenting your partner on their unique qualities—such as their kindness, intelligence, or sense of humor—can make them feel valued and cherished. For example, saying, "I love how thoughtful you are; you always know how to make me feel better," highlights a specific trait that makes your partner special to you.

Expressing appreciation for everyday actions is another powerful way to convey love. Thanking your partner for their contributions, whether they are big or small, shows that you notice and value their efforts. This can be as simple as saying, "Thank you for making dinner tonight; it was delicious," or "I really appreciate you picking up the groceries; it helped me a lot." These acknowledgments not only make your partner feel appreciated but also encourage a positive and supportive dynamic in your relationship.

Active listening is a crucial component of verbal expressions of love. When your partner speaks, give them your full attention. This means putting away distractions, making eye contact, and responding thoughtfully. Reflecting back what they've said, such as, "I hear you're feeling stressed about work," shows that you are engaged and empathetic. This kind of attentive listening validates your partner's feelings and fosters a deeper emotional connection.

Sharing your own feelings and experiences is equally important. Being open and vulnerable with your partner can enhance intimacy and trust. Instead of keeping your emotions to yourself, express how you feel about your relationship and your partner. For instance, saying, "I felt so proud of us when we worked through that disagreement," or "I feel incredibly lucky to have you in my life," opens up a space for mutual emotional sharing and understanding.

Storytelling can also be a powerful tool in expressing love verbally. Sharing memories of special moments, recounting the story of how you met, or discussing significant experiences you've shared can reinforce your bond and remind your partner of the journey you've been on together. For example, reminiscing about a memorable vacation or a particularly meaningful date can rekindle the emotions felt during those times and strengthen your connection.

Humor and playfulness have their place in verbal expressions of love as well. Light-hearted teasing, inside jokes, and playful banter can bring joy and laughter into your relationship. These moments of shared amusement can relieve stress and create a sense of camaraderie and partnership. Just be sure that your humor is always kind and never hurtful, as the goal is to uplift and connect, not to demean or criticize.

Conflict and disagreements are inevitable in any relationship, and how you communicate during these times is critical. Expressing love verbally during conflicts can be challenging but is essential. Using "I" statements to express how you feel without blaming your partner can help maintain a constructive dialogue. For example, saying, "I feel hurt when we argue and I don't want us to be upset with each other," communicates your feelings without assigning blame. Additionally, reaffirming your love even in the midst of a disagreement, such as, "I'm upset right now, but I love you and want to work through this together," can help de-escalate tension and reinforce your commitment to the relationship.

Apologies are another important aspect of verbal expressions of love. When you've made a mistake or hurt your partner, a sincere apology can go a long way in healing wounds and restoring trust. A genuine apology involves acknowledging what you did wrong, expressing regret, and committing to change. For instance, saying, "I'm really sorry for forgetting our anniversary; I know it hurt you and I regret not being more thoughtful," shows accountability and a desire to make amends.

Finally, the language of love is not limited to romantic relationships. Verbal expressions of love are equally important in friendships, family relationships, and even professional connections. Telling a friend how much their support means to you, expressing gratitude to a family member for their kindness, or acknowledging a colleague's hard work can strengthen these bonds and create a more positive and supportive environment.

In summary, verbal expressions of love are a fundamental way to communicate affection, appreciation, and commitment in relationships. By incorporating daily affirmations, specific compliments, expressions of appreciation, active listening, emotional sharing, storytelling, humor, constructive communication during conflicts, sincere apologies, and extending these practices beyond romantic relationships, you can create a richer and more fulfilling connection with those you care about. Love is not only felt but also spoken, and the words we choose to express it can profoundly shape our relationships and enrich our lives. Developing a habit of verbal expressions of love is a continuous journey that requires mindfulness and intention. As relationships evolve, so too must our ways of communicating. One effective approach is to set aside dedicated time each week to reflect on how you've expressed love verbally and consider new ways to do so. This practice can help keep your expressions fresh and meaningful.

Nonverbal Communication of Affection

Nonverbal communication is a powerful and often subtle way to express affection, playing a crucial role in how we connect with others. It encompasses a wide range of behaviors, from facial expressions and body language to touch and spatial proximity. Understanding and mastering nonverbal communication can deepen relationships, as these silent signals often speak louder than words.

One of the most immediate and impactful forms of nonverbal communication is eye contact. When you look into someone's eyes, you create a direct and intimate connection. Eye contact can convey a multitude of emotions: love, interest, comfort, and even desire. Maintaining eye contact during conversations shows that you are engaged and present, making the other person feel valued and understood. However, it's important to balance eye contact to avoid making the other person feel uncomfortable or scrutinized.

Facial expressions are another vital component of nonverbal communication. A genuine smile can instantly convey warmth and affection, breaking down barriers and inviting a positive response. Smiling, much like eye contact, has a contagious effect, often prompting others to smile back and creating a shared moment of happiness. Similarly, frowns, raised eyebrows, and other facial cues can communicate concern, empathy, or even displeasure, allowing you to express a wide range of emotions without saying a word.

Touch is perhaps one of the most intimate forms of nonverbal communication. Human touch has the power to comfort, reassure, and express love in ways that words often cannot. Simple gestures like holding hands, hugging, or a gentle pat on the back can convey deep affection and support. The key is to be mindful of the other person's comfort level and cultural norms, as touch can be perceived differently across various cultures and individual preferences.

Body language provides a wealth of information about our feelings and intentions. Open and relaxed postures, such as uncrossed arms and legs, signal receptiveness and approachability. Leaning slightly toward someone while they speak shows interest and engagement. Conversely, closed body language, like crossed arms or turning away, can indicate disinterest or discomfort. Being aware of your own body language and reading others' can enhance your ability to communicate affection nonverbally.

Proximity, or the physical distance between people, also communicates nonverbal messages. Standing or sitting close to someone can indicate intimacy, trust, and a desire to be near them. On the other hand, maintaining a greater distance can signal a need for personal space or discomfort. Understanding and respecting spatial boundaries is essential, as too much proximity can be perceived as intrusive, while too much distance can seem aloof or disinterested.

Gestures, though often subtle, can significantly enhance nonverbal communication. Small actions, like a thumbs-up, a wave, or a gentle nod, can convey agreement, encouragement, or acknowledgment. These gestures can reinforce verbal messages and provide clarity and emphasis. However, it's important to be aware of cultural differences in gestures, as meanings can vary widely across different regions and societies.

Nonverbal communication also extends to how we present ourselves and our environment. Personal appearance, including clothing, grooming, and overall demeanor, can send strong messages about how we feel and how we wish to be perceived. Dressing neatly and appropriately for an occasion can show respect and consideration for others. Similarly, creating a welcoming and comfortable environment, whether it's a tidy home or a well-organized workspace, can communicate care and attention to detail.

The use of silence in nonverbal communication is often underestimated. Silence can be a powerful tool, providing space for reflection, understanding, and emotional connection. In moments of shared silence, people can feel a deep sense of togetherness and empathy. It's important to recognize when silence is appropriate and how it can complement verbal communication, allowing emotions to resonate without the need for words.

Expressions of affection through nonverbal communication are not limited to romantic relationships. In friendships, family dynamics, and even professional settings, these silent signals play a crucial role in building and maintaining connections. A reassuring hug for a friend going through a tough time, a smile of encouragement to a colleague, or a comforting hand on a family member's shoulder can all communicate support and love effectively.

Nonverbal cues can also help navigate and resolve conflicts. Maintaining calm and open body language during a disagreement can prevent escalation and promote a more constructive dialogue. Avoiding aggressive gestures or facial expressions can help keep the conversation respectful and focused on resolving the issue. Nonverbal communication can thus be a powerful tool in de-escalating tensions and fostering understanding.

To improve your nonverbal communication skills, it's beneficial to practice mindfulness and self-awareness. Pay attention to your own nonverbal signals and how they might be perceived by others. Observing and learning from the nonverbal cues of those around you can also enhance your ability to interpret and respond appropriately. This ongoing practice can lead to more effective and authentic expressions of affection.

In addition to being aware of your own nonverbal communication, it's essential to develop the ability to read and respond to the nonverbal cues of others. This requires empathy and attentiveness, as well as an understanding that these cues can be subtle and context-dependent. By tuning into the body language, facial expressions, and other nonverbal signals of those you care about, you can better understand their needs and emotions, allowing for more meaningful and supportive interactions.

Nonverbal communication is also influenced by individual differences and personal histories. People have unique ways of expressing and interpreting affection based on their past experiences, personality traits, and cultural backgrounds. Being sensitive to these differences and adapting your nonverbal communication accordingly can help build stronger and more respectful relationships.

Incorporating nonverbal communication into your daily interactions can also enhance the depth and quality of your relationships. Simple acts like maintaining eye contact during conversations, offering a genuine smile, or giving a reassuring touch can make a significant difference. These small gestures, when done consistently and sincerely, reinforce your verbal expressions of love and create a more holistic and impactful way of connecting with others.

To sum up, nonverbal communication of affection encompasses a range of behaviors that convey love, support, and understanding without the need for words. By mastering eye contact, facial expressions, touch, body language, proximity, gestures, personal presentation, and the use of silence, you can enhance your ability to connect deeply with others. These silent signals, when used mindfully and empathetically, can strengthen relationships, resolve conflicts, and create a more loving and supportive environment. As you become more attuned to nonverbal communication, you will find that these subtle yet powerful expressions of affection can enrich your interactions and foster deeper connections with those you care about. Developing a keen awareness of nonverbal communication in your daily life also means recognizing the contexts in which these cues are most effective. For example, in moments of heightened emotions, such as during an argument or when someone is experiencing stress, nonverbal communication can provide a calming presence. A gentle touch on the arm or a supportive nod can help de-escalate tension and convey empathy when words might fail or be misinterpreted.

Love Language Compatibility

Understanding love language compatibility is crucial for fostering deep and meaningful relationships. Love languages, a concept popularized by Dr. Gary Chapman, describe the different ways people express and receive love. These languages include words of affirmation, acts of service, receiving gifts, quality time, and physical touch. Recognizing and adapting to your partner's love language can lead to a more harmonious and fulfilling relationship.

Consider the story of Sarah and John, a couple who initially struggled to connect on a deeper level. Sarah's primary love language was words of affirmation, while John's was acts of service. Sarah often felt unloved because John rarely expressed his feelings verbally. Conversely, John felt unappreciated because Sarah didn't acknowledge his efforts to show love through his actions. Their relationship improved significantly once they understood each other's love languages. John began to verbally affirm Sarah more often, and Sarah started to recognize and appreciate John's acts of service. This simple shift in understanding led to a profound transformation in their relationship.

Words of affirmation involve expressing love and appreciation through spoken or written words. Compliments, encouraging words, and expressions of gratitude can make someone who values this love language feel cherished. For instance, telling your partner how much you appreciate their support or how beautiful they look can significantly impact their emotional well-being. Simple phrases like "I love you" or "I'm proud of you" can go a long way in reinforcing your bond.

Acts of service are actions taken to show your love and care. This love language is about doing things you know your partner would appreciate, such as cooking a meal, running errands, or taking care of household chores. These acts demonstrate your commitment and willingness to make your partner's life easier. It's important to remember that the sincerity of these actions matters more than their scale. Even small gestures, like making a cup of coffee in the morning, can speak volumes.

Receiving gifts is a love language where the symbolic value of a gift expresses love. It's not about the materialism but the thoughtfulness behind the gesture. For someone who values this love language, receiving a gift, no matter how small, can be a tangible reminder that they are loved and thought of. Gifts can range from flowers and chocolates to a handwritten note or a surprise outing. The key is to choose gifts that resonate with your partner's tastes and preferences.

Quality time involves giving someone your undivided attention. This love language is about being present and engaged with your partner, whether through meaningful conversations, shared activities, or simply spending time together without distractions. For someone who values quality time, the most important aspect is the connection and intimacy that comes from being fully present. Turning off your phone, making eye contact, and actively listening can make your partner feel valued and important.

Physical touch is a love language that involves expressing love through physical affection. This can include holding hands, hugging, kissing, or any form of physical contact that conveys warmth and intimacy. For someone who values physical touch, these gestures provide a sense of security and love. It's important to note that physical touch should always be consensual and respectful of your partner's boundaries.

Compatibility in love languages doesn't mean that both partners must have the same primary love language. Instead, it's about understanding and adapting to each other's preferences. Consider the case of Emily and Daniel, who had different love languages but learned to appreciate and respond to each other's needs. Emily valued quality time, while Daniel's primary love language was physical touch. By making an effort to spend more uninterrupted time together and incorporating more physical affection into their daily routine, they were able to strengthen their bond and enhance their relationship.

To identify your and your partner's love languages, start by observing how each of you naturally expresses love. Pay attention to the ways you seek affection and the actions that make you feel most loved. Taking a love language quiz can also provide insights into your preferences. Once you understand your love languages, communicate openly with your partner about what makes you feel loved and appreciated. This mutual understanding can help you both make intentional efforts to meet each other's emotional needs.

Practicing love language compatibility involves more than just recognizing your partner's love language. It requires a commitment to regularly expressing love in ways that resonate with them. This might mean stepping out of your comfort zone or developing new habits, but the effort is worth it for the sake of a stronger and more loving relationship. For example, if your partner's love language is acts of service, you might need to prioritize helping out with tasks even if it's not your natural inclination. Similarly, if they value words of affirmation, you might need to practice verbalizing your appreciation more frequently.

Challenges can arise when partners have different love languages, but these differences can also provide opportunities for growth and deeper connection. One common challenge is feeling unappreciated when your love language is not being met. It's important to communicate these feelings to your partner without placing blame. Approach the conversation with empathy and a willingness to understand their perspective. For instance, instead of saying, "You never say you love me," you might express, "I feel most loved when you express your feelings verbally."

Another challenge is maintaining balance and reciprocity in expressing love. It's essential to ensure that both partners feel their love languages are being acknowledged and valued. This requires ongoing effort and communication. Regularly check in with each other to discuss how you're feeling and whether your needs are being met. These conversations can help you both stay attuned to each other's emotional well-being and make any necessary adjustments.

Adapting to your partner's love language also involves being mindful of their personality and preferences. For instance, someone who values quality time might prefer quiet, intimate settings over crowded, noisy environments. Tailoring your expressions of love to suit their individual tastes can enhance the impact of your efforts. Similarly, being aware of your partner's boundaries and comfort levels is crucial, especially when it comes to physical touch or acts of service.

In addition to focusing on your partner's love language, it's important to recognize and express your own needs. A healthy relationship involves a balance of giving and receiving love. Be open about what makes you feel cherished and appreciated, and encourage your partner to do the same. This mutual exchange fosters a deeper understanding and connection.

Love language compatibility is an ongoing journey that requires patience, effort, and communication. As you navigate this journey, remember that the goal is not perfection but progress. Celebrate the small victories and improvements in your relationship, and be patient with each other as you learn and grow together. By committing to understanding and honoring each other's love languages, you can build a stronger, more resilient, and more loving relationship. By embracing love language compatibility, you're fostering a relationship that thrives on mutual respect and understanding. Relationships are dynamic, constantly evolving entities that require regular attention and care. As you and your partner grow and change, so too might your love languages. Being attuned to these changes and maintaining open lines of communication will help ensure that your relationship remains strong and fulfilling.

Maintaining Affection over Time

Maintaining affection over time is a fundamental aspect of sustaining a healthy and fulfilling relationship. In the early stages of a relationship, passion and excitement often come naturally. However, as time goes on, couples may find it challenging to keep the spark alive amidst the demands of daily life. By intentionally nurturing your relationship and prioritizing affection, you can ensure that your bond remains strong and vibrant.

Consider the story of Michael and Laura, who have been married for over twenty years. In the beginning, their relationship was filled with spontaneous dates, heartfelt conversations, and constant physical affection. As they navigated the challenges of raising children, building careers, and managing household responsibilities, they noticed a gradual decline in their expressions of love. Recognizing the need to rekindle their connection, they made a conscious effort to reintroduce regular date nights, surprise gestures, and meaningful conversations into their routine. This shift not only revitalized their relationship but also deepened their emotional intimacy.

One of the key strategies for maintaining affection is to prioritize quality time together. In the hustle and bustle of everyday life, it's easy to become preoccupied with work, chores, and other obligations. However, setting aside dedicated time for each other can strengthen your bond and create lasting memories. This might involve scheduling regular date nights, weekend getaways, or even daily moments of connection, such as enjoying a morning coffee together or taking a walk in the evening.

Physical touch is another powerful way to maintain affection over time. Simple gestures like holding hands, hugging, or cuddling can convey warmth and love. Physical touch releases oxytocin, a hormone that promotes bonding and reduces stress. Even in long-term relationships, these small acts of affection can have a significant impact on your emotional connection. Being mindful of your partner's preferences and boundaries is essential, ensuring that physical touch is always comfortable and welcome.

Communication plays a crucial role in sustaining affection. Open and honest conversations about your feelings, desires, and needs can help you stay connected and address any underlying issues. Regularly expressing appreciation and gratitude for your partner can also reinforce your bond.

Compliments, words of encouragement, and expressions of love can make your partner feel valued and cherished. For example, telling your partner how much you appreciate their support during a challenging time or acknowledging their efforts in maintaining the household can go a long way in fostering affection.

Surprise gestures and acts of kindness can also help keep the romance alive. These don't have to be grand or extravagant; even small, thoughtful actions can make a significant difference. This might include leaving a love note in your partner's lunch, planning a surprise date, or doing something special to show you care. These gestures demonstrate your ongoing commitment and thoughtfulness, reminding your partner that they are loved and appreciated.

Shared experiences and activities can also enhance affection. Engaging in hobbies or interests together can create opportunities for bonding and fun. Whether it's cooking a meal, taking a dance class, or exploring a new hiking trail, shared activities can bring excitement and variety to your relationship. These experiences create positive memories and reinforce your connection.

Conflict resolution is another important aspect of maintaining affection over time. Disagreements and misunderstandings are inevitable in any relationship, but how you handle them can significantly impact your emotional bond. Approaching conflicts with empathy, patience, and a willingness to understand your partner's perspective can lead to healthier and more constructive resolutions. Avoiding blame and focusing on finding solutions together can strengthen your relationship and prevent resentment from building up.

Maintaining affection also involves nurturing your own well-being. Taking care of yourself physically, emotionally, and mentally can positively influence your relationship. When you feel good about yourself, you are more likely to bring positive energy and affection into your interactions with your partner. This might involve engaging in regular exercise, pursuing personal interests, and seeking support when needed.

Consider the example of Emma and David, who found that their busy schedules left little time for each other. They decided to make small changes to prioritize their relationship. They started by setting aside one evening each week for a date night, during which they would disconnect from their devices and focus solely on each other. They also made a habit of expressing appreciation daily, whether through a compliment, a thank-you note, or a simple "I love you." These intentional efforts helped them maintain their affection and deepen their connection.

Another strategy for maintaining affection is to keep the element of surprise and spontaneity alive in your relationship. While routines and predictability can provide stability, introducing occasional surprises can add excitement and novelty. This might involve planning a surprise weekend getaway, trying a new activity together, or simply surprising your partner with their favorite treat. These unexpected moments can reignite the passion and remind your partner of the excitement you felt in the early days of your relationship.

Maintaining affection over time also requires a commitment to personal growth and learning. Relationships are dynamic, and both partners will inevitably change and evolve. Embracing these changes and supporting each other's growth can strengthen your bond. This might involve setting shared goals, exploring new interests together, or encouraging each other to pursue individual passions. By growing together and individually, you can maintain a sense of connection and fulfillment.

It's important to recognize that maintaining affection is an ongoing process that requires effort and intention. There may be times when external stressors, such as work pressure or family responsibilities, make it challenging to prioritize your relationship. During these times, it's crucial to communicate openly and support each other. Acknowledging the challenges and working together to find solutions can help you navigate difficult periods and emerge stronger as a couple.

Reflecting on the journey of your relationship can also reinforce affection. Taking time to reminisce about shared experiences, milestones, and cherished memories can remind you of the love and connection you share. Looking through old photos, revisiting meaningful places, or simply talking about your favorite moments can evoke positive emotions and strengthen your bond.

In long-term relationships, it's natural for the initial intensity of romantic love to evolve into a deeper, more stable form of affection. This mature love is characterized by a strong sense of companionship, trust, and mutual respect. Embracing this evolution and appreciating the unique qualities of mature love can help you maintain a fulfilling and affectionate relationship.

Ultimately, maintaining affection over time involves a combination of intentional actions, open communication, and a commitment to nurturing your relationship. By prioritizing quality time, physical touch, communication, surprise gestures, shared experiences, conflict resolution, and personal growth, you can keep the spark alive and ensure that your bond remains strong and vibrant. Remember that every relationship is unique, and what works for one couple may not work for another. The key is to stay attuned to your partner's needs and make a continuous effort to express your love and appreciation. Maintaining affection over time is an art, a delicate balance of effort, empathy, and adaptability. It requires both partners to be active participants in the relationship, continuously nurturing the bond that brought them together. As you navigate the complexities of life together, here are a few additional strategies to consider:

Develop rituals of connection. These are small, regular habits that reinforce your bond. For example, you might start each day with a hug and a brief chat about your plans, or end each day with a few minutes of reflection and gratitude. Rituals create a sense of stability and belonging, serving as daily reminders of your commitment to each other.

Embrace the power of touch in everyday interactions. Physical affection isn't limited to intimate moments; it can be woven into your daily routine. A gentle touch on the arm, a kiss on the forehead, or sitting close together while watching a movie all contribute to a continuous expression of love. These small gestures can have a cumulative effect, keeping the connection alive even during busy or stressful times.